SUMMARY & ANALYSIS

OF

WOMEN ROWING NORTH

NAVIGATING LIFE'S CURRENTS
AND FLOURISHING AS WE AGE

A GUIDE TO THE BOOK
BY MARY PIPHER

NOTE: This book is a summary and analysis and is meant as a companion to, not a replacement for, the original book.
Please follow this link to purchase a copy of the original book: https://amzn.to/2LFvvzE

TABLE OF CONTENTS

SYNOPSIS

Aging gracefully involves 'rowing' up the river (a physical, mental, and emotional choice to participate in this life until the end). *Women Rowing North* is about cultivating emotional resilience through the twilight years, choosing an attitude conducive to happiness and continued growth.

There are four parts in twenty chapters which cover the challenges of aging, the skills to understand how women can grow old well, the companions they need on the journey, and the perspective on their own mortality, which guides their actions and decisions along the way.

Part One covers ageism, lookism, caregiving, loss, and loneliness. Part Two talks about the skills women need for this time of life—understanding themselves, skillful choices, community building, managing narratives, and gratitude. Part Three is about long-term loving relationships that bring stability through interdependence. Part Four discusses authenticity, enhanced perspectives, and bliss.

Pipher has interviewed hundreds of women in her time as a therapist, lecturer, and author. She draws on these records, sharing her own experience throughout the book. The four main time-lapsed interviews are for specific women; Willow, Kestrel, Emma, and Sylvia.

It's a narrative about making the aging journey transcendent as we head toward 'the land of snow and ice.'

PART 1: CHALLENGES OF THE JOURNEY

CHAPTER 1: A NEW STRETCH OF THE RIVER

"My body would age; my soul would expand." (Pipher, Chapter 1, p.25)

Every life stage is difficult, but especially for women who are entering the teenage years, like her grand-daughter, Kate, or the golden years in what Mary calls, the 'young-old' and then the 'old-old' stages.

Key Takeaway: Change comes rapidly, and women can adapt or fossilize.

There are two choices when this time of life presents such enormous challenges—adapt or wither. Those who adapt learn to navigate the new circumstances (the tired body, the myriad of losses, the pain) with grace and energy. Those who wither complain all the time, become self-absorbed, and stop growing as they forget that life is still full of adventures waiting to happen.

Loss is inevitable. It's also necessary for continued personal growth so vital in the twilight years. Only with coming to terms with loss do we learn to appreciate what we already have and to hold on to what we value the most.

The time of life facing those 'over the hill' is full of paradox—loss and satisfaction, wisdom and illness, vitality and the inability to move as quickly as before. Attitude is 'almost everything' to staying present and taking life as it comes (the good and the bad).

Key Takeaway: Willow is introduced.

Willow was the daughter of Russian immigrants who was still active, working, and full of life at seventy-two. She has always worked with people in a social work setting, deriving meaning and pleasure from her dedicated workdays and long hours.

Her second husband, Saul, whom she married in her fifties, had expressed a desire for her to slow down (to retire or travel or work half-days). Her greatest fear, though, was to lose the work she loved so much and to stagnate into old age. An eighty-year-old director was a bad marketing strategy for her nonprofit organization, so she knew that change was fast approaching.

CHAPTER 2: THE LAY OF THE LAND

Chapter Two explores the ideas of ageism—the prejudice against older women from without, and within. Old age isn't fun, especially in a society that values youth and beauty over anything else. Even Hollywood reflects how invisible older American women are in the society they have helped to birth and shape.

Key Takeaway: Three ways to claim power and secure respect for older women.

Mary is incredibly inspired by *Two Old Women* by Velma Wallis, a true Athabaskans story about women who were left behind but eventually saved their tribe from starvation. They proved their worth beyond anything expected within their community, through tenacity and a conscious decision not to give up.

Older women can find this same respect by doing these three things:

1. Take responsibility for educating others about the lives of older women and refuse to criticize yourself or accept negative remarks about your age.

2. Be an advocate for women of all ages, changing policies, standing against stereotypes, and lobbying for equality and recognition.

3. Talk to everyone, engaging meaningfully with people of all ages.

CHAPTER 3: THE WORN BODY

Sagging bodies and a less attractive reflection in the mirror can have a deep impact on sexuality and many other things as women age. The key to surviving this life stage is to be adaptable.

It's a time when you work harder to maintain your health but suffer more ills. The pain will always be there, but the rewards are great when you find a new equilibrium and embrace a full and happy life once more.

Key Takeaway: Sylvia is introduced.

Sylvia is married to Lewis, with one daughter, Lenore, who is a drug addict (current whereabouts: unknown). Sylvia is saddled with her two grandchildren, grief for her lost daughter, financial troubles, arthritis, excess weight, and a broken marriage relationship as she and Lewis diverge with their own troubles.

Key Takeaway: Kestrel is introduced.

Kestrel is a hard nut, with a tough exterior and an even tougher personality. She has inherited her father's alcoholism, only has casual relationships, and has succeeded in a career in information technology. She is a member of Pride and is angry at how her body is starting to let her down.

Her doctor insisted she stop drinking a bottle of red wine every night (due to osteoporosis), and Kestrel was livid. The thought of her body breaking down, however, was enough for her to stop (without any help from places like Alcoholics Anonymous). Her lifestyle has changed, though her abstinence is difficult to maintain with the company she keeps and the deep-set loneliness that lingers from her upbringing.

Key Takeaway: "Healing packages" are possible to create for ourselves.

Doctors often prescribe a 'healing package' of treatments, suggestions, lifestyle changes, and different approaches to ailments and trauma. It is possible for us to create these for ourselves, too.

Doctors often frustrate older women endlessly, not understanding (or bothering) about the reality of daily life when our bodies are falling apart, and society is watching.

Like Sylvia, a younger doctor's suggestions may be completely unsuited to the harsh reality. How could she exercise more and change her diet with no money, no time, and two grandchildren to look after for her drug-addicted, absent daughter?

Kestrel, too, was infuriated by her doctor's suggestions to stop drinking wine (her favorite activity, socially and medicinally) for the sake of her bones—even though it was a medically-sound opinion.

CHAPTER 4: INTENSITY AND POIGNANCY

Mary reflects on the bittersweet qualities that make old age such a precious experience. So much complexity resides within the days, months, and years that pass too quickly.

Poignancy seems the only way to describe the emotions of this time, for example, yet, it is somehow inadequate to describe the nuances—the 'library of feelings' within us.

Key Takeaway: Emma is introduced.

Emma is an Irish redhead, who has been married to Chris for forty-five years. They have three children, all married and then divorced, with four granddaughters. Emma was a second-grade educator until she retired three years ago.

She loves spending time with her grandchildren, especially as she realizes how quickly they have grown.

Key Takeaway: Mortality fosters gratitude.

When their long-time Scottish friend came to visit, the magnitude of the moment was almost too much to bear. They had known each other for decades, shared intimate secrets, and thought of each other as family. Now, he was too old and frail to do the trip again. It would be the final goodbye.

A looming death acts as a magnifier of small beauties, bringing tremendous gratitude to the minutiae of each day. People suffering from terminal diseases describe the clarity they experience, and the happiness they grasp when they realize time is running out. It's a great lesson in focus.

CHAPTER 5: CAREGIVING

Caregiving is a massive undertaking for anyone, let alone elderly women for whom the task is arduous and physically demanding. So many women find themselves in this situation, though, be it for their partners or parents. It is often an extension of their lifetime of giving care to their children and others, and it can be rewarding—but it can be excruciatingly painful and depressing, too.

Key Takeaway: Willow cared for Saul when he was diagnosed with Parkinson's disease.

When Willow was at the height of her busy career and enjoying it thoroughly, Saul was diagnosed with a degenerative illness that was already in mid-stages and was bound to worsen quickly. She was devastated. She wondered if it would hurt her career, test her personally, and cause problems in their marriage if she couldn't care for him as expected.

Slowly, though, she adapted. They talked through things, struggled through changing routines, and changed the way they interacted as Saul's health called for more hands-on care. She became a better wife and caregiver, more patient, less guilty, and happier in the role as she grew to know her own capacity for love and selflessness.

Key Takeaway: Caregivers often neglect self-care.

Caring for others can often be thankless and trying, with forty percent of caregivers suffering from depression and admitting that it is a highly stressful endeavor, even if they volunteered for the job. Aging parents can be demanding and relentless, for example, as their mental and physical health deteriorates.

It's vital for caregivers to set boundaries, and to do things that bring rest and restoration into their busy lives. Our relationship with a spouse that needs care changes, too, and it isn't easy.

Self-care is not an option, but an essential part of caring for someone else, especially where your own physical and mental health are at stake. Boundaries are necessary and set the tone for a healthy and meaningful period of caregiving where you need to be around long-term for the other person.

CHAPTER 6: SWEPT AWAY

The chapter explores the philosophy of hospice, which urges people to accept death and face it head on. It also discusses the nuances of grief, sharing stories to illustrate how loss can stall us in different ways.

Key Takeaway: Grief does not necessarily heal completely—it morphs and fades.

Grief is its own animal and every person experiences it uniquely. The point is to grow through the grief, to allow yourself to feel it fully, and then to decide what you will do with the clarity that it brings. It's a wake-up call waiting for a transcendent response, which helps us appreciate life more.

For widows, in Mary's experience, the second year is often harder than the first, since by then everyone (including themselves) expects them to feel better. They often don't, and then wonder what they're doing wrong. It can evoke disappointment, rage, frustration, and disillusionment.

CHAPTER 7: LONELINESS AND SOLITUDE

The discussion turns to the complexities of loneliness, which is so prevalent to the human condition. People feel lonely in crowded rooms, teenagers feel misunderstood, children feel unheard, and adults cope by embracing distraction.

Older women, who have often worked hard all their lives at everything else, start to realize the importance of meaningful friendships when they start to slow down.

What do we do when we isolate ourselves intentionally, and then feel lonely? Those with the right attitude reach out and connect with others, even if it's making a new friend in their late seventies. The others wither, alone in their apartments, in a constant state of confusion, loss, desperation, and sadness.

Key Takeaway: Kestrel is lonely.

Kestrel has embraced a life of solitude on the back of an early childhood of trauma and disconnect. She is in limbo between wanting more from her romantic pursuits and habitually shying away from intimacy. She's confused—why is she lonely when she has chosen to live this way.

It's taking a toll on her, highlighting her sobriety with insomnia, anxiety, and anger. She has a tumultuous relationship with her partner, constantly pulling away before slowly drifting together again. Kestrel knows it isn't sustainable, but she's never learned to trust anyone, so she doesn't know the remedy for her pain.

PART II: TRAVEL SKILLS

CHAPTER 8: UNDERSTANDING OURSELVES

For women who have taken cues from others about who they are, it can be difficult to discover late in life that they don't know themselves very well. Dealing with pent up emotion, like anger, is vital to leading a well-adjusted life, especially as women age.

Key Takeaway: Time management and learning to say 'no' is vital.

Women are constantly under pressure to cater to others, answering the needs of those around them with selflessness and enthusiasm. Learning to say 'no' is the first step to acknowledging that only you can meet your own needs adequately. It's a life skill that women don't often hone (or even realize they are missing) until they are well into their golden years.

Key Takeaway: Anger requires expression.

For most women, anger is an 'unladylike' emotion that is repressed and denied wherever possible. It resides in our bodies, killing our souls, and manifesting in myriad other problems, like depression. It's better to express it, however you need to, verbally saying what you need to say out loud, or physically pounding out the rage (without hurting anyone else) until you can think clearly.

For Emma, this was a long and arduous road, and she didn't realize at first how much tension she carried in her life. She was a positive, bubbly person, but her people-pleasing ways eventually came to a head. She went to therapy, and learned how to set boundaries with her husband, her daughter, and the other meaningful relationships in her life.

Emma learned to say 'no' and it released the long-standing anger and tension inside of her—she became a different person as she embraced who she really was and what she wanted from life. She learned to protect herself by saying 'no,' to know and value her physical, emotional, and spiritual needs.

CHAPTER 9: MAKING INTENTIONAL CHOICES

As women navigate the 'river,' there is power in choosing an intentional direction for themselves. It is a turning point, an attitude change, to stand up and do what your heart and mind know is right for you.

It's never too late to become intentional about choices, time, relationships, and your wants and needs. By Mary's definition, being wealthy is about being content with your choices, not being financially stable. She is wealthy in her experiences, loving relationships, and anything else she 'collects' intentionally in her life.

Key Takeaway: Willow quits her job.

As Saul's Parkinson's progressed to the point of him not being able to get out of bed by himself, Willow suddenly decided that it was time for her to stop working at the organization she loved. Her colleagues were ready when she voiced her decision, and she was probably the most surprised of everyone by her resignation. She continued to be a support to the new leader, but ultimately, her focus now rested with Saul, his health, their home, and their relationship.

Willow felt free. For the first time in her life, she also felt happy, knowing that she was exactly where she wanted to be, doing exactly what she needed to be doing to stay true to herself. It was impossible to believe that her work, which so defined her, was now gone, and yet, she was more fulfilled than ever.

Her attitude was the key to making the transition successfully. It helped her become self-aware and confident, strong enough to face what lay ahead for her and Saul.

Key Takeaway: Kestrel cares for her mother.

Kestrel chose to care for her mother in the summer she was diagnosed with Stage III cancer. It was a time of tremendous personal growth for Kestrel, as she learned about herself and confided in her partner.

She was surprised by the ease of sharing intimate details with someone else and she started looking at the world with new eyes—still managing to stay sober through the pain she felt over her mother's suffering.

CHAPTER 10: BUILDING A GOOD DAY

Life is nothing without 'small treats' that allow us to change gears and refocus. A cup of coffee with a friend, a nap, a new game—all are necessary to keep us from leaning too far in one direction and overbalancing. It encourages us to pace ourselves, especially as we are readjusting to our aging bodies.

Key Takeaway: Sylvia finds healing in small changes to her schedule.

Tired and stressed, with little sleep and demanding custodial grandchildren, Sylvia decided to visit one of the pain clinics recommended by her doctor. She was desperate but didn't expect much from the appointment. When she met Megan, the therapist, she talked for an hour and found herself surprised by the advice she received.

Megan suggested Sylvia talk to someone, rate her stress level each day in a journal, and return to her beloved swimming twice a week. The suggestions were simple, yet seemed doable, and Sylvia vowed to follow the advice.

Soon, she realized that her life was changing—she was happier, sleeping better, healing her relationship with Lewis, enjoying her grandchildren, and forming friendships at her church group.

Key Takeaway: "Minimizers" have reasonable expectations and are generally happier people.

When we set our expectations high, we are usually disappointed. Not to say that we shouldn't have any expectations at all, but we need to learn to be flexible and realistic about what the situation can do for us. It's best to live in the moment, enjoying it fully, because no 'magical future' is beckoning—it's here and now that counts.

The key to crafting a 'good day' is start it well and end it well. Wake up with positive thoughts and gratitude for the moments which have passed and are to come. Close the day off with good thoughts, too, as you bask in all the beauty, love, and wonder that punctuated the life you led today.

CHAPTER 11: CREATING COMMUNITY

The chapter explores the idea of community building, where action (in this case, to help others) is the only way to bring hope and purpose to life after retirement.

Key Takeaway: "Action is the antidote to despair."

For people with more time on their hands, involvement in meaningful pastimes is more important than ever. Whatever the area of interest, calculated action and focused use of experience and wisdom is vital to a more fulfilled life—not only for the aged. Advocacy is a powerful form of engagement with the world around us.

It is also important to keep a balance between passion and rest, as it is in every stage of life.

A group can achieve more than an individual and can lighten the blow of failures that are sure to come when we take up causes to make the world a better place. Many voices are better than one and acting for the good of our communities connects and strengthens us.

OBSOLETE SPELLING OF RESPLENDENT CPKG

CHAPTER 12: CRAFTING RESPLENDENT NARRATIVES

Much of our ability to adapt to life's changes comes from the will and opportunity to modify our stories. When we tell a more positive, encouraging or beautiful story about who and what we are, we are uplifted, and so are our listeners. We use our old stories to craft new ones, and those fresh narratives move us forward onto hallowed ground.

Key Takeaway: Sylvia, Emma, Willow, and Kestrel all crafted better stories.

Sylvia was able to reconnect with her husband, appreciate her two resident grandchildren, and find joy in the moments she spent outside of the home with exercise and church groups.

Emma took strength from her husband, Chris, appreciating his humor and learning to look at her situation differently.

Willow made the choice to embrace her time with Saul. The weaker he got, the more jovial he tried to be, and she was astounded by how much fun they had together. She didn't miss work, because she had decided that this was their precious time with her husband she could not pass up.

For Kestrel, it was more difficult to adapt after a lifetime of hiding behind the walls constructed around her heart. Her mother's illness was a catalyst for change, however, and slowly, but surely Kestrel crafted her story into a more positive one. She even agreed to a long-term commitment with her partner—an unprecedented move from the long-time loner.

CHAPTER 13: ANCHORING IN GRATITUDE

Developing our 'gratitude skills' is a healthy habit that will help us to see the beauty amid the tragedy.

People like Sally set the bar high for living a life of gratitude and contentment. Sally is fully engaged in the small things that make her life amazing, not focusing on her severe health issues or her other struggles. Contentment prompts us to see the details and appreciate them.

When we are grateful, our perspective on suffering changes drastically. People who have suffered greatly also tend to be the most grateful and content of everyone. They are more compassionate, more loving, and more appreciative of life in general.

PART III: THE PEOPLE ON THE BOAT

CHAPTER 14: TRAVEL COMPANIONS

As women walk through the later years, they discover the true value of female friendships—through the good and the bad times. Some friends meet in high school or college, others meet when they have children the same age. Soul mates are often friends overnight and remain friends, easily, no matter the circumstances.

Sustaining these friendships is like any other relationship—it takes work and a little bit of effort. In modern society, connection isn't emphasized, and friendship takes a backseat to technology, career paths, and pastimes. Women have forgotten how important it is to invest real time and effort into face-to-face relationships with other women, to carry each other through life with warm hands and hearts.

For Mary, Betty was a pivotal influence in her life—a community builder who hosted events and initiated interesting commonalities on which people could bond. People like Betty understand the value of maintaining friendships, too, for shared memories, and a smile that lights up when you walk into the room.

CHAPTER 15: CO-CAPTAINS

Marriages are unique relationships that are lengthening with longevity as populations age. Emma's marriage to Chris has taught them many lessons about the value of relationships, including how to let the other share without judgement when needed.

For many who are in long-term relationships, it is difficult to describe the beauty of being close to someone—protected and loved by another being in the most intimate way possible. It is a gift to be cherished.

Key Takeaway: General guidelines for a successful marriage.

- Emotional and social space is crucial for individual growth and mutual happiness.

- Each partner takes charge of their own relatives (visits, gifts, decisions, and plans).

- We each choose the friends we want.

- We each make decisions about our own bodies.

- "Couple friends" can make life happier together.

- It is important to acknowledge what your partner has said, to show that you listened, and you care.

- Spouses need to adapt to a partner's changes, which is inevitable as we mature and develop new interests.

CHAPTER 16: THE LIFEBOAT OF FAMILY

Family is something we all need—desperately. It's the people who keep us warm when nobody is around, pay our bills when we are in a tough spot, and laugh with us whenever possible. It is only as life wanes that we realize how much these family relationships define us and move us.

It becomes more important to know where we have come from as we get older, to know about the paths that have led to where we are and forged a way in the world before us. As we grow, we become the ancestors, forging paths for those who will come after us in the endless parade we call life.

Kestrel embraced time with her family the summer her mother died. They had a family gathering at her mother's bidding, enjoying games and meals, having fun together, and catching up. It was only through this interaction, late in life, that Kestrel realized how much she needed the family she was a part of, including Becca, her partner whom she had chosen as family.

CHAPTER 17: GRANDCHILDREN

Grandchildren are the light of our lives, tiny bundles of happiness and energy that reveal our capacity for loving another person. Sometimes, they are difficult, but when we make time for them, crafting special memory-building activities, it can be a most beautiful relationship.

Grandparents are 'cultural historians' teaching the next generation about where they came from by telling them about our own lives, our childhoods, the games we love, the historical events that shaped us, our values, and beliefs. We teach them what is important to us, modeling the behavior for them. We shape them with pointed questions that help them to mature, problem-solving in their complicated little lives.

The relationship with our grandchildren changes constantly as they grow. We adapt to their new interests as we mourn their quick development. We become those people who wait at the window and chat at the car making it hard for the family to leave after a visit.

It is a time to lend support to our children, not to pass judgement or force unsolicited advice on already tired parents. Enjoy life in the present and treasure the memories.

PART IV: THE NORTHERN LIGHTS

CHAPTER 18: MOON RIVER: AUTHENTICITY AND SELF-ACCEPTANCE

One of the gifts of old age is the freedom to be true to ourselves. There is no need for pretense or hypocrisy. We don't need to be bound by any obligations that push against our instincts.

For Willow, it was accepting her new role as caregiver to Saul, allowing herself to just be happy with the circumstances. For Mary, it was learning that it was okay to not be engaged in yet another self-improvement project. She gave herself permission to be content; just as she was in that moment.

Mary also had an epiphany on a Bahamas beach one holiday. She realized that her emotions didn't need 'prettifying' and that she could feel things as they came and went in her heart. Authenticity, finally, brought healing.

CHAPTER 19: THE LONG VIEW

As we move toward the light, we see ourselves and others with renewed perspective, perhaps over six generations at once. Older people have experienced more and know how to solve things (often as a result of encountering those situations in the past). They are also more connected in the continuity of time, which binds and shapes us.

Willow took pride in what she had achieved in her career, while appreciating her present role as caretaker and friend of her ailing husband. Sylvia looked upon Lenore's situation with mixed feelings but found joy in raising her grandchildren and giving them opportunities. Emma countered her bouts of sadness with the beautiful memories she has stored away over the years.

"We don't see the world as it is, but rather as we are." (Pipher, Chapter 19, p. 238)

Time is a healer because there is growth through adversity and the realization that we can take hard knocks.

CHAPTER 20: EVERYTHING IS ILLUMINATED

Bliss tempers our experience with beauty amid suffering. Our souls crack open so better things can displace the pain; joy, gratitude, happiness, peace, acceptance, and love. When we learn to embrace everything as it is, life is as good as it can ever be—every moment becomes precious.

EDITORIAL REVIEW

A deeply personal book which draws on her life and knowledge, Mary Pipher's *Women Rowing North* is a reflection on women growing old; as she does herself. She considers herself an 'average' person, telling a relatable story about cultural and social changes for aging women in America, yet she is remarkable in so many ways.

Mary has crammed a lifetime of wisdom into a two-day read, expertly weaving together the stories of her subjects, patients, and friends into a captivating tapestry. You get the impression of her sitting in a sunny room with a cup of tea and poignant photographs on a mantlepiece, smiling as she recalls the thousands of people who have taught her about the world. It's clear she appreciates the nuances of culture, and her words embrace diversity in a way that is truly inspiring.

The underlying tone is one of nostalgia, but also of unquenchable hope. The septuagenarian tackles life with determination, an unconventional poignancy, and as a natural encourager to her kindred spirits. Her narrative acknowledges hardships in the same breath that it insists upon tenacity.

It's obvious that she has sought spiritual meaning in many places during her life, never quite landing on religion as a stopping point. Her life has been spent observing others, and this is the source of her stories and sage advice. A drive, a current, beneath her words carries us into honest and painful anecdotes, clarity of purpose, and the beauty of stoically facing death as it looms upstream.

Her message is that women need emotional resilience to navigate and flourish old age, and that this is mostly to do with attitude, and gratitude.

Some of the 'getting older' themes are well-known; the inevitable slowing down, choosing to be mentally sound when you're battling physically, being happiest when you're present in reality, and relying on friendships to keep you going. The 'cultural therapist' truly understands her topic—she has lived it and is living it—and it makes the story so much more believable. Maybe, we could all be like that at her age?

Much of the slow read evokes a sigh and an eye-roll, yet there is so much truth to be gleaned from the triumphs and failures of her countless human studies. If you've got the time to reflect on the hope and resilience, it's invaluable, and touching.

It's the slow beat of a drum in the conversations of older, wiser individuals. As ageism reigns, the elderly are marginalized, even resented, especially in cultures that do not value or care for their parents and grandparents. A younger generation may not appreciate the pearls of wisdom within this anthology of life, yet Pipher has thrown them before the pigs anyway, in the hope her message will be heeded.

"Nobody will protect you from your suffering. You can't cry it away or eat it away or starve it away or walk it away or punch it away or even therapy it away. It's just there, and you have to survive it. You have to endure it. You have to live through it and love it and move on and be better for it and run as far as you can...across the bridge that was built by your own desire to heal."—Cheryl Strayed

BACKGROUND ON AUTHOR

Mary Pipher is a fascinating and remarkable woman. A psychologist who has specialized in women, trauma, and mental health as it relates to culture, she is an experienced and confident mouthpiece for feminism and the empowerment of women.

Mary grew up in Beaver Creek, Nebraska. She was the child born in the 50s who grew up in 60s and landed in the middle of the Vietnamese War era when she was at college.

A Baby Boomer, she was hardworking and cannot believe how much the country has changed in just a few short decades. Even her own memories seem like echoes from another life that she has since left far behind. She believes, though, that women can 'master the skill of resilience' like we master cooking, driving, and yoga (Pipher, Chapter 1, p.17).

Mary also happens to be the author of more than nine successful books about the cultural and social themes that hold her interest (mostly about women). She has spent her life on various adventures—a daughter, big sister, wife to Jim, mother, grandmother to five, caregiver, lecturer, cultural anthropologist, clinical psychologist, and researcher.

Her role models are social activists: Alice Paul, Tillie Olsen, Grace Boggs, and, especially, Margaret Fuller.

OTHER TITLES BY MARY PIPHER

The Green Boat: Reviving Ourselves in Our Capsized Culture (2013)

Seeking Peace: Chronicles of the Worst Buddhist in the World (2009)

Writing to Change the World (2006)

Letters to a Young Therapist (2003)

The Middle of Everywhere: Helping Refugees Enter the American Community (2002)

Another Country: Navigating the Emotional Terrain of Our Elders (1999)

The Shelter of Each Other: Rebuilding Our Families (1996)

Reviving Ophelia: Saving the Selves of Adolescent Girls (1994)

Hunger Pains: The Modern Woman's Tragic Quest for Thinness (1988)

END OF BOOK SUMMARY

If you enjoyed this ZIP Reads publication, we encourage you to purchase a copy of <u>the original book.</u>

We'd also love an honest review on Amazon.com!

Made in the USA
Monee, IL
16 October 2020